THE ANGELS CARRIED ME

BETWEEN LIFE AND DEATH
FOR SIXTEEN MINUTES

To
Roselee
Nice that we got
to chat. I
hope you in Injoy
Edith M Pype
404-925-9987

THE ANGELS CARRIED ME

BETWEEN LIFE AND DEATH
FOR SIXTEEN MINUTES

EDITH M. PYE

iUniverse, Inc.
Bloomington

The Angels Carried Me Between Life and Death
For Sixteen Minutes

iUniverse books may be ordered through booksellers or by contacting:

iUniverse
1663 Liberty Drive
Bloomington, IN 47403
www.iuniverse.com
1-800-Authors (1-800-288-4677)

ISBN: 978-1-4620-4118-3 (sc)
ISBN: 978-1-4620-4119-0 (ebk)

Printed in the United States of America

iUniverse rev. date: 08/31/2011

Contents

"For He shall give his Angels charge over thee,
to keep thee in all thy ways."

Psalms 91:11 KJV

It's true; Jesus took the sting out of death!
I escaped death.

1 Corinthians 15:55 KJV

Acknowledgments

Telling my story has not been easy; sometimes very painful, yet at times so blessed to be able to share it. First, I want to thank God, the author and finisher of my faith. I would like to say thanks to my husband, Thomas Pye, who at the time was my friend. He stood by me through it all.

To my four children and their companions; Garfield and Rebecca Chambers, Gary and Julie Chambers, Tamatha and Monte Shiflett, and Greg and Wendy Chambers. I want to thank them for their support in every way.

To my grandchildren; their smiling faces and gentle touch brought healing and gave me courage to fight to live, especially my grandson Merle Chambers, who reminded me that I had told him I would write a book of how the angels carried me.

To my granddaughter, Marlene Pierce, for all the nights she pampered me by massaging my back, my broken leg and foot. She was my little helper and encourager.

To my granddaughter, Christen Chambers, and her Mother Wendy with all the help of typing and corrections and help on this book.

To all my family and friends who took the time out of their busy day to visit me and call, and brought me flowers and helped to bathe and dress me. Thanks.

To Debbie Webb at Short Cutz Beauty Shop in Griffin, GA, for keeping my hair washed and done and also for the benefit singing she prepared to help me with my finances.

To all the volunteer nurses, Barbara Kempson, and Jill Newton for coming to the house to nurse me and keep check on me.

To my daughter, Tamatha and son-in-law, Monte, for taking me in their home for seven months during my recovery.

I love you all and pray that God will return the blessing to each of you
In loving memories of those who have gone on before me: My dad, Clarence Adrian Seeley, my brother, Edward Lee Seeley, my sister, Myrna Marlene Seeley, who welcomed me with out-stretched arms. And especially to my children's dad Garfield Junior Chambers who passed after the accident.

Love,
Edith Mae Pye

Home place where I grew up.

My grandchildren

Our Kids

The Day My Whole Life Changed

"For he saith, I have heard thee in a time excepted, and in the day of salvation have I succoured thee; Behold, now is the accepted time; Behold, now is the day of salvation",

II Corinthians 6:2 KJV

Today is the day of salvation. We should wake up every morning of our lives falling on our knees and thanking God for life, health and strength. We should follow the spirit man instead of the flesh; for our flesh warfares against our spirit. So, whichever we feed the most is the one that wins.

I was suffering from depression, a spirit that many friends have confided to me about. I did not understand what they were feeling until I had to face it myself. I had no idea how much this could devastate your whole life. I had gone through a lot of life changes and at the age of 55 felt alone. I knew I was loved by my family and friends, but there seemed to be something missing.

It was Wednesday, March 31, 2003, somewhere around 6:30 am. I climbed out of the bed as usual, not knowing the day would be anything out of the norm. A day I would face a giant called death. Something we all have to face one day, "If Jesus doesn't come before." This day would change my life completely. The small things in life we take for granted, things so simple, such as taking a shower, brushing my teeth, fixing my hair and dressing myself, such things as putting on my shoes or making my own bed. These were the things I did that morning that someone else would have to do for me in the months to come.

I often try to recall what I had for breakfast that morning, as it was my last meal for several weeks resulting in my losing thirty pounds. Did I ask God to bless that meal, or did I get in a hurry and forget to pray? Did I run out the door before I got down and talked to God? Did I ask Him to take care of me and guide me in the way that I should go? Or, maybe I was on the phone with someone.

I do remember my plans were to go and visit some of my grandchildren. I spent several hours with them and headed back home, or to a place where I lived. Home is a happy dwelling place if happiness is coming from the heart.

You see, if you ever have had a close walk with God and later in life allow sin to come into your life, something is always missing. No matter whom you are or who you are with or what you do—your life will be miserable! And mine was!

The bible says, "Good understanding giveth favor; but the ways of a transgressor is hard," Proverbs 13:15 KJV. Sure, I prayed every day, went to church and had been fasting. I really believe that is why God spared me that day. He knew my heart and I knew sin could not enter into Heaven, small nor great.

I believe God warned me to get everything under the blood, for just a few nights prior I had a dream, more like a nightmare. I even shared this with a friend. I know we should tell a dream just as a dream, so I did. However, it haunted me and would not leave my mind and I had a situation that I knew I had to fix that was far more powerful than I and it was resolved that very day. You see, nothing is too great for God and he will allow the hedge to be removed and allow things to happen for our own good.

Being different growing up, I always knew I had a special calling on my life that caused me to carry a fear of God within me. It's not always easy to do the right thing, but it pays to pray.

Weeping overtook me as I was driving. Blinded by the tears and the hurt, I pulled over to sit in a gas station parking lot until I was able to drive home. Later that afternoon I was lying across my bed, resting and making plans to ride to Fayetteville, GA to have supper with my friend, Tom. He knew something was wrong with me and he asked if I felt like driving. "Yes," I replied, "I just don't feel like being alone."

Here I go, running out the door again. I ask myself now, "Did I pray?" The most important part of our life is to stay in touch with God at all times. We never know when we are going to be faced with tragedies of life.

I walked out and closed the door not realizing that it would be the last time ever to see the things I was leaving behind. I climbed into the car and pulled out for a journey of no return. The last thing I recall is somewhere around five miles down the road, the evening sun came over my windshield and blinded me.

As I was coming around a curve, into a little town in Williamson, GA, I failed to see what was in front of me. From that moment, my life would be changed forever.

Pictured: Edith Pye before the accident.

Pictured: Edith's car before the accident

The Accident

"Weeping may endure for a night, but joy cometh in the morning,"

Psalms 30:5 KJV

Sometimes it's hard to talk about hurtful memories and try to explain the events. I guess sometimes we tend to block out the pain. We would rather not talk or write or even think on these things. But, I choose to allow my heart to override my mind and tell the facts. "Greater is He that is in me than he that is in the world," I John 4:4 KJV.

I want others to know and realize that without the presence of God we have no chance for survival. I know I would not have had a chance without God. He was my only source of strength, blood supply and present help during the impact. Often we fail to remember that moms and dads, husbands and wives, and even children can only go so far with us. Jesus said, "Lo, I am with you always, even unto the end of the world," Matthew 28:20 KJV.

It seems like a dream, then again, a nightmare—something that could happen so quickly. One minute I am seeing clearly to drive, the next minute, the evening sun pours over the windshield of my 1999 Plymouth Voyager van and I'm blinded. Suddenly, there was a deadly sound and a pain in my chest that took my breath away. I felt as though a huge bull had charged me. All I could think was, "God, help me and forgive me!" Then, everything went silent and my thoughts were, "I'm dead!"

KJV Romans 8:28 tells us, "And we know that all things work together for the good to them that love God, to them who are called according to His purpose," Believe me; it has worked out for my good.

When I was able to look and see what happened, I saw a pickup truck directly in front of me. Smoke was boiling out of it. It was so close; it looked as if I could look inside. I remember thinking, "Help! Somebody get me out of here before I burn up!" Something else has grabbed my attention; some type of white liquid was running from it.

I found out later that it was milk. The person I hit had just stopped by the store to buy two gallons. The milk had busted and was spilling out on the highway. It's amazing the very minutest of small details that someone can recall during a time of destruction.

I saw a man that I recognized, standing outside near my van. He was so still, and he looked scared. He had come to hear me sing on several occasions. I just knew that he would help me. I will never forget his reply as I begged him to pull me out. SILENCE!!!!! I pleaded, "Don't let me burn up, please!" He just backed away slowly and never said a word to try and comfort me.

Later, I figured he must have been in shock also for after my recovery I saw him again and he told me he was afraid and knew I was in critical condition.

I looked for my cell phone which I thought was in my passenger seat but realized it had fallen into the floor. I reached down to pick it up; it was at this point that I realized the van motor had pushed through the dash of the van and rested on my right foot.

I have no idea how many bones I shattered. As the old saying goes, it looked like a million. They were all exposed. I must have gone into shock because I reached down to pull off my knee high, only to discover the bones in my lower leg were holding it tightly in place.

I grabbed the phone and called my daughter, Tamatha, and Marlene, my granddaughter, answered. She quickly gave her mother the phone because she was too afraid to speak. I was able to tell her I had been in an accident and had broken my foot and when she asked me where, I could not remember.

As I was talking to Tamatha, a patrol officer arrived on the scene. He opened the door and I handed him the phone.

He explained to my daughter the location of the accident so she could find me. Paramedics arrived also.

One had climbed into my back seat and asked me where I was hurting. He checked to see if my neck was broken. He pressed on, "Where do you hurt?" I replied nowhere. He asked if I was having any difficulty breathing and I replied, "It just knocked the breath out of me, I will be alright."

I mentioned my foot and another medic came to stabilize it and stop the bleeding. "Do you hurt," he asked. At that point I was going in and out of consciousness.

The paramedics continued to talk to me in an attempt to keep me awake. Finally, they strapped me onto a stretcher and removed me from what I would describe as the pits of hell.

As I look back to remember, I pray for anyone that would have to go through any type of experience like that.

My daughter had come to the scene of the accident and a wave of peace came over me just knowing she was there. She took charge of the situation.

I do not remember the ride to the Spalding Regional Hospital, but I do remember the comforting voices of the paramedics.

Tamatha informed them that I often had panic attacks. One medic replied, "It's more than that, her blood pressure is dropping rapidly, which is a sign of internal injuries."

I do not know to this day what did the most injury; my seatbelt or my airbag. My liver was lacerated, the main artery to my colon was pulled and my other organs were severely bruised. I believe in wearing seatbelts for it's the law and we are to obey the laws of the land.

Now a question is probably arising in your mind as to whose fault it was for the accident. It was mine. I really had a hard time forgiving myself for hurting someone else.

I did have the privilege of meeting the gentleman that I hit. His name is Mark and I did ask for his forgiveness and thank God, he did forgive me! He told me his wife was pregnant when the accident happened and because God gave us grace, he named his baby girl Grace.

His mother had been out of church for many years and because of the accident, she dedicated her life back to God. We all know God has a way to get our attention.

These are pictures of what my van looked like
after the accident.

My Short Visit to the First Hospital

I can't remember too much about the first hospital I came to which was Spalding Regional in Griffin, GA. What I do recall wasn't good, except the presence of my two older sons. I know other family members and friends were there, but for some reason the rest is elusive to me.

Looking up through my pain and fear, seeing Garfield, my oldest son, I felt comforted, at the same time scared, for I did not want him to watch me die and I knew that's what was happening. With strength I really didn't have to spare, I replied "if you ever prayed in your life you better pray now" I knew he wasn't in church but I trusted in my heart he would pray and touch God for me.

I must have been coming in and out of consciousness, for now I am hearing a police officer reading me my rights. I could not understand why or what was going on, except I had been in a wreck and it was serious.

Suddenly, my son Gary, with an angry voice, was telling the officer, "Get out of my mother's room now!" He did learn later it was against hospital policy the way the officers handled it.

The officers questioned me about taking drugs because a half of pill was found on the passenger's seat that I had laid there hours prior to the accident. The medication was for depression.

I know a lot of tests were done on me to find out what was going on. The nurses and doctors were trying to figure out what was going on with me and with this being a small town hospital, that is not equipped to handle anyone with serious problems, left my family with a decision they would have to make quickly, for my life depended on it. So they took action and had me immediately airlifted to Atlanta medical Center in Atlanta Ga. I don't recall any of it.

My Flight
with the Angels

The bumpy ride on the stretcher and the loud sound of the helicopter ringing in my ears blocked some of the memory of what was really going on around me. I realized I was the center of attention and somewhat didn't like it. It made me realize that my condition was serious. On takeoff the medics we're giving me blood and taking my vitals.

My voice was weak and my hands were trembling but I managed to reach up and touch the young man's face and asked what my vitals were. "60/30 please don't die on me!" was his response.

Through my confusion of what was going on and also coming in and out of consciousness I confused him with my baby son, Greg. Thinking it was him, I found comfort to hold on. Even with all the strength I could muster up I could not resist the Death Angel.

There are two things in life we have to face, life itself and death. I began to feel a peace come over me and something happened that would change my life forever.

Without pain and fear, I heard the last voice I would hear while my spirit left as if I were floating out of my body into the clouds. I knew this must be it, as I saw my loved ones who'd gone on before me.

I saw my dad, who had been gone ten years, my oldest brother Ed, who was my childhood hero, who only three years ago died with cancer, and I saw my baby sister, Marlene, who was only thirty-one when she was taken from us by a man who was obsessed with her and couldn't have her. They looked like angels dressed in white.

I saw the smiles on their faces, telling me to come home. I got so close that I could almost touch them I realized that going home would be great but then, I saw the faces of all my children and grandchildren. I knew I wanted to stay with my dad, brother and sister but, at the same time my family here on earth pulled me back, so I asked them to release me and let me go back to spend more time with my family.

I did not know how long I was gone before my spirit entered back into my body. All I heard was, "We've got her back," by one of the medics in the helicopter.

An angel appeared to me, it was the Angel of Life. I heard him say, "I will carry you for sixteen minutes between life and death", immediately to confirm the time, I heard the pilot call to the Atlanta Medical Hospital saying, "We'll have her there in sixteen minutes."

The bible talks a lot about angels. Mark 1:13 KJV says, "And he was there in the wilderness forty days tempted of Satan and there was with him the wild beast and the angels ministered unto him." We all know the word does not change, he is the same today, yesterday and forever, he cannot lie, his promises are given conditionally. We should do all we know to do and know that God will do the rest.

The next sixteen minutes are lost memory to me. When we landed, I remember being moved from the helicopter into the halls heading to the Trauma room to face another scary experience.

My sister Marlene Thompson

My oldest brother Ed Seeley

My dad Clarence Seeley

Trauma Room

Lights, lots of lights and long hallways, was the view from the helicopter to the trauma room, then to the Intensive Care Unit. I could hear voices, but, no faces to go with them.

Great speed on the stretcher was very important, for I was losing blood faster than the paramedics were giving it to me. I was listening to the instructions of one of the doctors, later to learn that it was Dr. Walker from East Point, GA, who would be the one to take over and be in charge of my life. He said to everyone that I was in shock and would not respond to anyone or anything, but, I could hear every word that was said, and I knew everything that was going on around me.

The lights were so bright that they would not allow my eyes to open. I had no strength to reply to anyone. Dr. Walker replied, "Save her foot, someone hold it in place because the circulation is very poor, we want to try and save it if possible."

Somewhere back in my mind I was trying to figure out every thing that was going on. Time was moving very fast, yet going so slow. It seemed like a lifetime in a matter of minutes.

I remember the bones were hanging out of my foot and my leg was broken. But, they were more concerned about the hemorrhaging inside. "Get her open immediately, we are losing her." "Someone read her vitals!" Their reply was "very poor and dropping." Lets get her open, were the last words I would remember for almost a week.

All this time that was going on, I was trying to say, "Help! Some one help me! Don't cut me open! I'm awake!" It's always important when you are in the midst of a trauma, to be very careful of every word that you speak, and try to control your emotions. It's better to be absent than to talk doubt. Immediately my body went into shock. So they had to rush and get in and out immediately.

Time was very important they had to do exploratory surgery, not knowing where I was losing so much blood. After finding that the main artery to my colon had been detached and my liver was lacerated, and my other organs were bruised, I ended up 8 pints short of blood, that meant a blood transfusion.

Many complications would follow, such as infections that would lead to my stomach being opened, leaving me with open wounds for several months and lots of surgical hernias. They had told my children to wait because I may not make it. Thank God, He already knew my future and had everything under control.

I was asleep for one week before anything could be done to my crushed foot and broken leg. I was losing circulation of blood in my leg and it was starting to die and the doctors told my children that I was going to lose my foot because they decided that gangrene would eventually set up and they were certain that it would eventually take my life. Praise God, that my children would not allow this to happen. Their reply was, "When mom wakes up, she will tell you what to do."

My family from Indiana had been notified of the accident. You need to know my family to understand all the tragedies I have been through. A lot of emotions are shared within my family. Sometimes overdramatized to say the least.

They did not tell my mother how serious my condition was, they tried to hide it from her to keep her sane on the drive down to Atlanta, GA. When she got to the hospital, my children let her and my sister Lodema go in first.

When they entered the ICU to see me, I was told later that they had ran out to tell the nurse that that was the wrong room, it was not me. I looked like I had weighed 300 pounds. I vaguely remember my mom saying, "Edith, it's mom, you're going to be alright", she spoke faith. Hebrews 11:1 KJV says, "Faith is the substance of things hoped for the evidence of things not seen."

Then I heard my sister say, "This is Lodema, I'm here." Those would be the last words I heard until I had a visit from the Holy Ghost.

Rev. Donny and Barbara Boyd came to visit me, all I know is a sound came into the room like on the day of Pentecost. Filling my room and shaking my body, mind and spirit. Act 2: 1-2 KJV. The Holy Ghost began to speak: through a minister and replied, "You will live and not die. Your work is not finished". Oh how wonderful to hear and feel that supernatural power that caused me to open my eyes, and start to live again.

Pictured left to right are my family from Indiana: me, Linda, Mary, Doris, Lodema, Wayne, Mildred, Bennie, Patricia, James, Merle and my mom Jeanette Seeley.
These are my brothers and sisters who are left.

Ants, Ants, Ants

As the saying goes, cheaper by the dozen, well believe you me! Ants, the smallest people on earth, they stick together, and yes, by the dozens. If only family, friends, and church people would watch carefully and take heed. Ants are an example of working together. Remember, strength in numbers, and we will never lose a battle.

The Bible speaks of ants in Proverbs 6:6 KJV "Being small, but exceedingly wise, not strong, yet they prepare their meat for the summer."

I can imagine that is what they were doing the night I awoke in my bed, as I was being hurled out of my room, bumping into walls while the nurses were urgently trying to get me to another room before the ants crawled into my bed.

They were running up the walls, crossing window sills, scattered over the floor. Everyone had the same questions. Where did they come from? Why this room? What are we going to do? I was too weak to ask any questions, so I just lay still and listened, terrified of something so small yet so mighty.

I felt so intimidated because I was helpless. If only we would remember, "Greater is He that is within us than he that is in the world," fear would no longer have a place in our lives.

With the condition of my body that had been so weak, I had no fight in me. If you have ever been so sick that you felt you would have to die to get better, you know how I was feeling at that point. But when all else fails, that's when God takes over. "There is no temptation, taken you but such as is common to man; but God is faithful, who will not suffer you to be tempted above that you are able; but will with the temptation also make a way to escape, that you may be able to bear it," I Corinthians 10:13 KJV. That is the way, the only way, to get over or through our problems.

Flowers, Flowers, Flowers

I had so many flowers that were sent to me that the staff said they had never seen a room so full. There were roses of all colors. And just like the ants—dozens of them.

Plants—you name it, I received it. At the time, I could not fathom that so many people loved and cared about me. Thoughts raced through my mind like 'I must be really going to die or people really feel sorry for me."

You know how the devil loves to play with our minds. Remember the saying, 'actions speak louder than words.' so I chose to believe and accept it as love.

Prayers, Prayers, Prayers

I am thankful for all my friends and families prayers and what it brought me through.

While growing up, I heard more praying than anything else. I remember my dad taught us children to pray. The Bible says, 'Pray without ceasing. You must understand verse 16 also; it says 'rejoice evermore,' I Thessalonians 5:16-17 KJV. So if we rejoice and pray, something is sure to happen.

Prayer was a necessity in our family. You see, we did not have medical insurance so we could not run to the hospital every time we needed to. So, we prayed, and we prayed. We prayed until we got an answer. It did not always come how or when we thought it should, but it always came, and on time.

Talking to God was just as real as talking to my Dad! Always remember—prayer works. My time when I was released out of the ICU to the main floor is very shady. I do not remember much, for pain and medication did not allow me.

I remember visitations, but only a few. I do, however, remember all the prayers. So always remember prayer works!

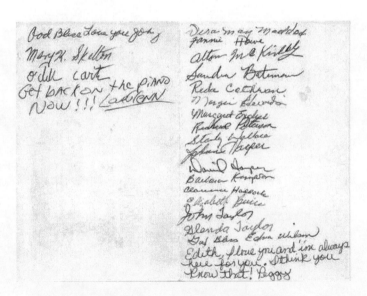

The get well card from all my friends here.

My Set Back

I began to heal and it looked like I might get to go home. Suddenly things began to fall apart.

One evening, Tamatha and Tom just happened to visit me at the same time. I was so tired of lying inside four walls that I had cabin fever. Someone suggested they put me on an elevator and push me outside. The only way to get me outside was to get me in a rolling chair that let out into a bed. This would not be easy for me, or anyone else for that matter, because I could not be of any help at all.

They managed to get me outside, and I remember that the air felt so good. It was breathtaking. As soon as the cool air hit my body I began to chill. So badly they had to get me back inside immediately.

As soon as they got me back into my bed I began to vomit so forcefully. I think it scared Tamatha. She bolted down the hallway to get help. It didn't seem to bother Tom, a Vietnam veteran; he had stood by many dying men. He was able to help by holding me and holding a trash can at the same time to catch the gross infection that was making me so sick.

The nurses ran into the room and discovered I was running a high fever of 105 degrees. I had set up a staph infection as well as pneumonia.

Now I am almost back to where I started—a very sick woman. Doctors started running tests to find out what type of infections I had so that they would know how to treat me. They also started giving me breathing treatments three times a day and pumping antibiotics into my body.

By this time my family was so worn out that they decided to stay home, which was a Sunday and rest.

Tom did not know this and he had the same idea as they did. He later said he wanted to give room to my family. So this leads to me spending the day alone.

As I lie there, unable to get out of bed or even turn over on my own. For the first time, I began to feel sorry for myself. It was at this point the four walls began to close in on me.

The doctor persisted with tests to ensure that the infections were clearing up. I really felt I needed someone there to hold my hand. Yes, it sounds childish, but remember, the trauma of the accident and all the setbacks; how all this had effected my nerves and I just was not a strong person at this time.

Tom had perfect timing that day. He showed up just before they began running tests and believe me, he was more than welcome. In fact, that may have been the turning point in which he won my heart. No one but God knows what that meant to me.

The next day, the doctors came in and told me the infection was gone, and that they would release me to a rehabilitation center.

Get well card from my family and friends in Indiana

My Journey Home

Well, my big day has come. All that I had been going through seemed to fade away. If or when you have an experience like mine, you will know what I am talking about.

Pain is something no one likes to remember. We, as human beings, push it so far back into our minds because it hurts too bad to keep it in focus! Now I have to meditate deeply to remember that this really happened to me. At the same time, it is a nightmare you would never wish on your worst enemy; something you never fully get over.

So, the doctors said I could go home. Of course, not my home though. My daughter-in-law, Wendy, moved all my things out of that little apartment in Zebulon, Georgia. She gave away what she was unable to move, and stored the rest of my things. Months later I was able to see what I had left.

My ride home was scary, yet so inviting. Tom was there to help Tamatha put me in the back seat of her car. They laid pillows down for my head, foot and leg to keep some of the pain down.

I'll never forget—as the car began to roll away from the hospital, fear gripped my heart. Tamatha must have known this because she started talking to me immediately.

I laid so still, staring into the sky, trying to keep my mind off the accident while she started up the conversation.

With her soft voice, she replied, "Mom, I know you have been wondering if you have a brain tumor like your brother Ed. Well, it's a fact that you don't. The doctors ran every kind of test there is on your head to see if you had any damage. All the tests came back negative," she informed me.

My brother, Ed had just passed away, leaving me with a void feeling and I was so glad that she was right. I had been to doctors with questions about it but did not want to go through all the testing. Wow, what a painful way to find out.

After traveling about an hour, we made it! With this success came another challenge—getting me out of the car and into the house.

Oh, yes, Tom followed us to make sure we made it. He picked me up and helped me into the house.

I did not know if he would disappear after my return home or continue to see me. What a way to win someone's heart. He did not give up. He became a big part of my healing process.

He visited me after work; sometimes to eat supper or to even take me out, but, only after I had healed enough to get into a car safely. He would pick me up with his arms, set me in my wheelchair and roll me outside to put me in the truck.

Well, if we care for someone, we will go beyond the call of duty, and he did.

My first trip to church was Easter Sunday. I was very swollen from the surgery, but Tamatha had bought me the prettiest blue dress. She dressed me, and fixed my hair.

Monte, my son-in-law, would have to take me down the steps backwards to get me to the car. I was so scared he would drop me! "Thou wilt keep in perfect peace, whose mind is stayed on thee; because he trusted in thee," Isaiah 26:3 KJV. He did not drop me.

I was so uncomfortable at church because I didn't want anyone looking at me. I probably felt worse than I looked.

After church, we took a trip to watch the grandchildren hunt eggs. That was the day I asked for my rings back. They had been taken off my hands by paramedics because my body was swelling.

My daughter-in-law, Julie, had given them back to me. One of the rings was missing; a one-karat diamond, I had just bought two weeks prior. I had paid $2,500.00 for it. I felt sick knowing a person could do that to someone in my condition. I didn't buy insurance for it, so I had to pay off a ring I didn't have.

Oh, well. I am so blessed—God has been good to me! Honestly, I can't complain.

Lots of time was put into taking care of the wounds that were still open. I had to be careful to keep the external affixation, a set of rods on the outside an area of broken bones to stabilize them long enough to heal. It couldn't be taken off until I had my final surgery.

Pictured left to right: Marlene, Monte,
Andrew, Tamatha and Carson

My Trip back to the Hospital

Hospitals are not a place where anyone likes to be, especially, not for a long length of time. We know sometimes, it's the only place to be to get help for our earthly bodies when you are in the shape I was in. But we all know it's wonderful to be released and go home

My first three major surgeries took place during my first two weeks stay in the Atlanta Medical Center. Upon release, I still had an affixer connected from my foot to my knee on my right leg. It was very painful and uncomfortable. My right foot had staples in it where they had done skin graft. Gangrene had set up because my condition was too critical to operate and fix the problem.

The doctors asked my children to sign a release paper that would allow the doctors to amputate my foot or it would take my life.

My oldest son, Garfield, told them no, that when I was awake I could sign the paper myself. He firmly believed that I would be able to walk again.

Thank God, he did not sign the paper. Someone's faith reached heaven for me seven days later.

As I was on my way to surgery, I barely remember my daughter walking beside me explaining where I was going and why I would have skin graphs taken from my right hip.

She explained that it would replace the skin that had rotted away from my foot. I fell back off to sleep I have no clue how long.

Every day, the doctor would come in and check it to see if everything took, and to his amazement, everything was healing fast.

A staph infection began to set up in my stomach from where they had to do the exploratory surgery. Dr. Walker, who had performed the surgery, had to reopen me and leave me open to heal slowly in order for me to go home temporarily. I had to have a nurse and a lot of medical attention.

I was told I had to go to a rehabilitation center for a while. I hated that thought and pleaded with my daughter to please take me home and take care of me.

My daughter, Tamatha, took on a huge responsibility, one she did not deserve. She has a husband, two children and a full time job, one where she travels a lot and now me!

She would clean and dress my wounds twice a day. A nurse would come and check in on me. She always had someone to come and bathe me. She had to be my mom at times.

When we went back to the doctor to prepare for my last surgery, I got so nervous that she had to calm me down.

The doctor explained how he would have to put a rod through my heel up into my leg connecting with bolts and screws shorting my leg one half inch. In order to keep me from falling, they would have to replace every bone from the bone bank in my ankle.

They tried to remove a bone, but, I was too frail. I even made a stupid statement that I didn't want it done, of course, I didn't have a choice.

I went to Piedmont Hospital in Atlanta, GA. The heavy load fell back on Tamatha! My sons had missed so much work they had to go back and try to catch up.

I am very thankful for Tamatha's employer who gave her time off or else I would have been in trouble.

My friend Tom told me he was going to be out of town, and could not be there. I realized then that I did not want him to go. I think that I really started to depend on him being there for me. But I could not allow him to know how I felt.

The night before my surgery, I got so depressed and scared. I caught myself crying; not wanting to even talk to anyone, I went to bed.

The phone rang and it was my family from Indiana. It was bad news, news that would take my mind off myself and cause me to pray.

My two nephews had an accident on a four wheeler leaving one of them paralyzed. His spine was permanently damaged.

It was hard for me to sleep that night not knowing what was ahead for him. I knew it would be a long healing for both of us. We both would be in surgery at the same time but different states.

I know it was hard on my mother that morning. She had been raising him ever since his mother, my sister, Marlene, had died.

The day had come that I would sign myself back into the hospital for a three to five hour surgery that would allow me to walk again.

Tamatha and I were sitting in the waiting room waiting for them to call me to the operation room. I looked up and to my surprise there stood my friend Tom. I just knew my day was going to be better, and it was.

The next 24 hours would be very painful, but just knowing that it would be over made it worthwhile. When I awoke, to my surprise, Tom was still there.

The doctor said the operation was successful and the next day I would be able to go home.

My nephew, Justin Seeley, was left in a wheel chair for the rest of his life. We are still hoping for a miracle for him.

From left to right: Ashley, Patricia, Mary, Ed, Me,
Derek, Justin, mom, Merle, Bennie

A Song

"Oh, sing unto the lord a new song for he has done marvelous things, his right hand, and his Holy arm hath gotten him the victory."

Ps. 98-1 KJV

God always prepares a way to help us through or out of our afflictions. 1 Cor. 10-13 KJV. "There has no temptation taken you but such as is common to man, but God is faithful, who will not suffer you to be tempted above that you are able, but will with the temptation also make a way to escape, that you may be able to bare it." Some cry, weep, and mourn. Some even rejoice, but as for me, I write, mainly songs.

In my deepest trying moments, I grab a pen and paper. It doesn't matter what type of paper. Sometimes I will grab a napkin from the kitchen table, or a receipt of some type that I may find in my pocketbook.

Often times while driving down the road, I'll ask somebody to write for me. Sometimes I even write God letters. And as hard as it may be to believe, I even get answers. Ps. 100:2 KJV, "Serve the Lord with gladness; come before his presence with singing."

I started writing gospel music at the age of 14. I recorded my first song, Without You Lord, in 1977 when I was 29.

But the song that I wrote, Top of the Mountain, has provided me with more spiritual help than any other song I've ever wrote. I wrote this song in 1999, while on a church trip to Stone Mountain Ga.

The church group I was with rode the sky lift to the top of the mountain. I refused to go, because I had a fear of the ride. Sitting waiting at the bottom I looked up, and a thought came to me. I grabbed a pen and piece of paper. I had it finished writing before the church group returned back down from the mountain.

I ended up with one of the best blessings of my life. This song has blessed many people, especially my brother Ed, who passed in 2000, with brain cancer.

He would ask me to sit at the piano play and sing it for him. We never know what a song means to someone dying. Ps. 40-3 KJV, "and he hath put a new song in my mouth, even praise unto our God, many shall see it and fear, and shall trust in the lord."

After coming home from the hospital, I was on a lot of pain medication that was causing me to have a lot of panic attacks.

The first day I was left alone at the house, I had one. And I thought I was going to die, and then I started singing the song "Top of the mountain." I never had another Panic Attack. Ps. 98-1 KJV "oh sing unto the lord a new song for he has done marvelous things, his right hand, and his Holy arm hath gotten him the victory."

When my sister, Marlene was taken from us, my family handled it all different. She loved yellow roses, so I wrote a song, "D0 Yellow Roses Grow in Heaven?"

My dad, who had passed on two years later, sang a song called "Not my will, but thine, be done", so I incorporated those words into Do Yellow Roses Grow in Heaven. It seemed to comfort my family and many others that had gone through this same tragedy.

God has used the song Amazing Grace, all across the nation to bless and comfort many hearts! Ps. 96 KJV "O, sing into the lord a new song, sing unto the lord all the Earth." The Word tells us, one day we can sing a song that the angels will not be able to sing.

Me on the lawn of the recording studio in
Nashville Tenn. of my first album.

The back cover of my second album.

Healing

"A man to whom God have given riches, wealth and honor, so that he wanteth nothing for his soul, of all that he desireth, yet God giveth him not power to eat thereof but a stranger eateth it this is vanity, and it is an evil disease."

Ecclesiastes 6:2 KJV

To be healed means to be complete. There are so many different ways to be healed. The soul is the most important healing anyone can receive. "For God so loved the world that he gave his only begotten son, that whosoever believeth in him should not perish but have everlasting life." John 3:16 KJV.

Then there is the mind. We often get depressed; not being able to deal with what life deals us. But Gods word says, "Thy will keep him in perfect peace, whose mind is stayed on thee, because he trusteth in thee." Isaiah 26:3 KJV.

Of course, then there is the body which suffers many different diseases. "Is any sick among you? Let him call for the elders of the church and let them pray over him, anointing him, with oil, in the name of the Lord, and the prayer of faith shall save the sick, and the lord shall raise him up . . ." James 5:14,15 KJV.

Fact is, I needed all three of these healings. So I searched the Word and listened to other peoples testimonies of their healings, and it gave me courage to believe I would receive mine.

For God has no respect of person. What he does for one, he will do for another.

Some people love being sick, because that's the only way they get pity, and attention! We have to be willing and ready, to do what it takes, to be healed.

Forgiveness is the most important part. The Bible says, "Then said Jesus, Father, forgive them; for they know not what they do . . ." Luke 23:34 KJV.

I had a lot of hurt and unforgiveness, so I had to make a lot of things right with many people. Maybe, I had been hurt, but the main one I had to forgive, was myself.

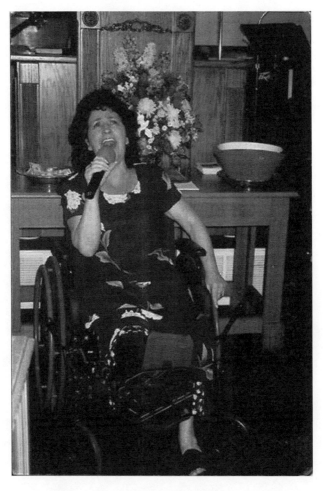

Me in my wheel chair singing for the Lord
at my benefit singing

Look Mom,
I Grew!!!!

"And the blind, and the lame came to him in the temple; and he healed them."

Matthew 21:14 KJV

I went to the bone doctor, Dr. Eric Furie, who is an orthopedic specialist that works on ball player injuries at the Northside Hospital, for a final checkup. It was very exciting because I knew he would be surprised to see what God had done for me, how I had healed and walked without a limp.

Dr. Furie told me that with my fused ankle it would change my step and could cause me to fall at times. This is why it was necessary for me to have my leg shortened one half inch. This would leave me four foot, eleven and one half inch on my right side and five foot on the left side.

Being short was never a problem because I was from a rather short family. My dad was only five foot nine inches and my mom was five foot three inches. I didn't like the idea of being shorter on one side than the other. But, God has a way to show his power and let the world know He is in control. "But Jesus beheld them, and said unto them, with men, this is impossible, but with God all things are possible." Matthew 19:2 KJV. Somehow through my weakness I was shown a miracle.

The doctor began to do an exam on me and asked me to take a walk for him down the hall and let him watch me to see how I was walking. I believe I stunned him.

He then asked me if he could do a video of me walking. He said that he would like to show other patients how there is hope. He knew in his heart it had to be an act of God that performed this miracle.

Dr. Furie measured my legs, and was surprised to see that my right leg had grown one and one half inch, and my left leg had grown one inch.

Before the accident I was five foot one inch tall. This just doesn't happen. Dr. Furie could not explain how this could happen, so he released me and said as far as he could see I did not need him any longer. This was seven years ago and I've never went back.

The next year, I went to Piedmont Medical Care in Fayetteville GA to have a yearly physical done. They always ask how tall you are. I told them I was five feet and one inch tall and I explained what had happen to me. The doctors were amazed as they looked back into my records. "For with God, nothing shall be impossible. "Luke 1:37 KJV.

My parents: Clarence and Jeanette Seeley

Shoes

Coming from a large family, shoes were always hard to come by. My daddy was a minister, traveling from church to church. Sometimes people would bless us with bags of shoes.

We would all dive in, in search for our size. Oh how happy it would make our day. We did not care that they were not new, even color or style, just so they fit.

As a teenager, I can remember, I used to have this same special dream, from time to time, climbing a huge mountain, covered with shoes and purses, reminds me of an Easter egg hunt.

We would run up the mountain and gather them up, but I always woke up before I came back down the mountain. Sounds like when God prepares a blessing and we never receive it. We can see it from a distance, but never receive it.

After getting married, I always seemed to notice all the women as they walked by. I liked to see what style or color shoe they wore. I suppose I still had that fantasy.

I started having children, and we also traveled in the ministry, full time. There wasn't that much money.

I'm not complaining because it was a wonderful life to serve God and see souls saved, healed and delivered. But when there was extra money, one of the children needed shoes. We always provided for them first and people were always giving me shoes.

They say history repeats itself, and it did for me. Out of the four children I was blessed with one daughter. When she got old enough to work, she made a deal with me, and believe me, I love deals. She said if I had lost 20 pounds, she would buy me a new wardrobe of clothes and shoes.

Now after waiting a lifetime, you better know I went for that special diet and lost that weight. She stuck with her promise. I was so proud. I had a water bed with 12 drawers underneath, and that's where I put my shoes, one to match each dress. My dream had finally come true. I was so thankful. I have found that when we are blessed, a spirit of jealousy always follows.

One of the women in the church accused me of just showing off. The Bible says, "Set me as a seal upon thine heart, as a seal upon thine arm; love is strong as death; jealousy is cruel as the grave; the coals there of are coals of fire which hath a most vehement flame." Song of Solomon 8:6 KJV.

I don't understand everything that happens but within six months my children and I went to a family reunion in Indiana. While traveling back home, we came through multiple tornados.

One of them was in Georgia. Lightning struck my house, blowing out the windows, and burning my house. Guess where the fireman said it struck? In my closet. It burnt up every garment I had, except one hanging in my car and the one I had on my back. And remember those shoes? They were also gone. The worst part, I had no insurance to cover the house, or any of my belongings. I never completely replaced my clothing or shoes, but God is faithful, he has never allowed anything to come upon us too hard for us to bear. 1 Corinthians 10 KJV, "He said he'll make a way for our escape." So God made a way for me to rebuild the house.

I almost felt like Job he said, "Naked came I out of my mother's womb and naked I shall return thither: the Lord gave and the Lord hath taken away, blessed be the name of the Lord." Job 2:21 KJV.

God hates pride, and sometimes I wonder if I might have had some. Shoes have always been some type of an attraction to me, so after the wreck, here I almost lose my right foot, but was blessed to keep it, I would never be able to wear high heels again. Thank God I can still wear shoes, and I still have two feet.

After my recovery, Tamatha took me shoe shopping again. This time it was no fun.

I was learning to walk again. I have one small foot and the other is large, swollen and painful, fused, and let's not forget ugly. I didn't want anyone to gaze or feel sorry for me; I just wanted to wear shoes again.

I tried on so many ugly special shoes. If it fit the left foot, I couldn't get it on the right one, and if it fit the right one, I would have to stuff tissue in the toe of my left shoe.

We finally found a pair to fit me. They were black Hushpuppies, ugly but pretty, if you know what I mean. I was so happy to be able to wear shoes. And guess what? The most expensive pair of shoes I owned for something that looked like that, $50. Looking back it is so funny but yet sad.

I went shopping for wedding shoes. For sure not black Hushpuppies. I would have a hard time finding the right color and style. I felt like the little woman in the Bible that had lost her precious coin, and I found them. They weren't black, they were beige, and they were dress shoes. They weren't heels, but they were nice.

It's been 8 years since the accident, and now we are in Helen, Georgia. The children asked Tom and I to go tubing down the river with them. If you have ever done this you will know what I'm talking about. There is a tree with lost shoes hung up on it that people have lost while tubing down the river, my son Garfield yells out, "Look mom, you need a tree like this in your backyard." He didn't realize the memories he brought back to me were good and bad. Paul said we ought to be content in whatever state we are in. I am happy to be alive, happy to wear shoes and walking, with or without shoes.

My granddaughter Marlene and I in our fancy dress shoes prior to the accident.

To Drive Again

"Yea though I walk through the valley of death, I will fear no evil for thou art with me, thy rod and thy staff, they comfort me."

Psalms 23 KJV

Fear often stops us from doing things in life we would love to do. Growing older, I have fought to overcome a lot of fears. We miss out on so many of the promises of God. To drive is something that everyone needs to do, if possible.

I have a nephew, Brent, who lives in Hendersonville Tennessee that is legally blind. He is one of the sweetest boys you will ever meet.

The one thing in life he wanted to do was the thing he was told he would never do, and that was to drive. My heart bled for him.

I asked him one day if he really wanted to drive then, come with me. I handed him my keys, got in the car, sat right next to him, and told him to drive.

Yes, he ran off the road. He even drove into the neighbor's yards. We would drive every time we got a chance until.

He became confident enough to go get special training, and then to an eye specialist. They made him special glasses, and today he is driving. Everyone told me I was crazy, but I believed in him. "They that sow in tears shall reap in joy." Psalms 126:5 KJV.

I never knew that one day someone would have to trust in me. After the accident, it was not promising that I would ever be able to drive again. I had fear of hurting someone else, but one day, Tamatha explained to me, that's why they are called accidents. It's something that can happen to anyone.

She handed me her keys, and told me to drive. It felt so good to drive after 5 months it ended the problem of someone taking me everywhere, and doing everything for me. Thank God I have overcome my fears, and I enjoying driving again.

My Love Story

"A time to love, and a time to hate; a time of war, and a time of peace."

Ecclesiastes 3:8 KJV

Love is a language created by God. It is designed so that people of all ages can understand it. Even a newborn baby can feel when they are loved.

It can be felt many ways—touching someone's hand; looking one in the eye; talking and spending time together, etc.

Love comes from God. That is why there is no respect of person, money can't buy it.

There is a big difference between lust and love. Many people fall for beauty and riches—soon to find out it is not real. Love will last, even after death. Song of Solomon 8:6 KJV says, "Love is strong as death."

Love can be blinding, Think, how a mother cannot see her children's wrong doings, and she will be the last to believe her children can do anything wrong. The Bible says, "Hatred stirrith up strife; but love covereth all sins," Proverbs 10:12 KJV. So, we learn the hard way because if it came too easy it would be too good to be true.

Love can heal, or it can kill. Just before the accident I had made a promise to myself that I would never fall in love again because it hurt too much.

I had a friend, and believe me—that's all he was. He was someone I could talk to, cry on his shoulder, and go out to dinner with.

We met through a gospel singing group my son Greg and his wife, Wendy, were in. They used to try and put us together; we both said no. They would always tease Greg about Tom being his new dad. I thought he was very nice for someone else, but, not for me.

Friendship love can and sometimes becomes true love. One night I was on my way to eat supper with Tommy Pye, and when I did not make it, he said he figured I must have stood him up. My daughter, Tamatha, calls him and she explained about the wreck and that I was being air lifted to Atlanta Medical Center.

At the time, she did not realize he would be there to stay for the long haul. Nurses thought we were married because he would sit in the ICU for hours on end. Sadly, I never knew he was there.

He told me he took my boys out to eat. They say the way to a man's heart is through his stomach, and it is. Another one is—'don't start something you can't finish.' I was really happy to know that the boys accepted Tom and did not try running him away.

Although, it is hard to believe because of the strong pain medication I was on, I thought I was hearing them make a plan on how to run him off. I even warned him about it but he replied, "No one will make me leave," and he did not.

Tom asked me to marry him while I was still in my wheelchair. Believe me I was not ready for that. My reply was, "Only if I learn to walk again."

If the truth be told, in the back of my mind I thought it would be a very long time, for my leg and foot felt completely helpless.

Tom tried many different ways to prove to me that I did not need the wheelchair. He even tried getting rid of it. Finally, I graduated to a three-legged walker. He tried so hard to prove I could walk without it. I ended up falling on the ground. Talk about upset—I was! But, he had already drawn a plan for me to be his wife, and believe me he was not to be changed by me or anyone else for that matter.

Then came the time to move on to a cane. It was wonderful to know I was close to walking. Well, as the song goes, 'my day will come.' It did!

I will never forget the day a very special friend of mine, Cathy Clower, took me to therapy. Well, guess what? They took my cane away. They left me in the middle of the floor without anything to lean on, and I started to fall. The therapist grabbed me and replied, "Try again. I promise I won't let you go." Through my fears—yes, I was so afraid but trust finally took over. I took my first step. I remember in an excited scream saying, "Watch me walk!" Unless you have been where I was, you can never know how whole I felt.

Well guess what else? Tom and I set a date. We were married October 24, 2003. Six months later, we learned that Tom had cancer.

This would be a true test of true love. After twenty-two days of radiation therapy, the doctors informed us he had many other illnesses.

God has given us strength and love. We have been blessed with a good marriage. Thank you Tom, for coming into my life.

Pictured left to right—Gregory, Christen,
Wendy, Holly and Greg, my son.

Pictured left to right—Julie, Garrison,
Gary—my son, and Tristan

Pictured left to right—Merle, Elijah, John, Rebecca,
Garfield—my son, Natalie and Garfield IV

An answered prayer he is to me;
My greatest blessing she'll always be.
And so this day we'll pledge our love
in front of friends and God above.

EDITH MAE HARPER

AND

THOMAS IRVING PYE

Honor us with your presence at
our wedding

on Friday, October 24, 2003

6:00 pm

West Sunnyside Congregational
Holiness Church
Corner of School & Patterson Roads
Griffin, Georgia

Please join us for a small reception immediately
following the ceremony.

My wedding invitation

Tom, me, Tom's mom, Tom's dad
and Tom's Sister Sandra

My oldest son Garfield giving me away to Tom

Tom and I after our "I do's"

When I Thought It Was All Over . . .

"For his anger endureth but a moment; in his favor is life. Weeping may endure for a night, but joy cometh in the morning"

Psalms 30:5 KJV

Never would I ever believe anything could happen that could be worse than the accident. We think we have got it bad, but when we look around there is always someone in worse condition than us. The bible says, "Many are the afflictions of the righteous; but the Lord delivereth him out of them all." Psalms 34:19 KJV. Although, we know God has it all in control, his love for us will cause him to pull back his hand of protection and allow us to go through things we don't understand.

Thanksgiving Day in 2006, Tom and I had gone to a thanksgiving dinner at his sister's house in Jasper Ga. Although we were having a good time, I had gotten a sick feeling in the pit of my stomach. So much so that I had to go lie down, and pray. I felt something wasn't right. The phone rang, and on the other end of the phone I hear a voice that is filled with fear and desperation. It was my sister, Patricia. Immediately, I knew it was bad. She was repeating over and over again, "Get a hold of yourself." Finally interrupting her, I said, "Tell me it's not Garfield," she said "Yes, there has been an accident, and it's serious." I asked "Is he alive?" She said, "We think so, but really we don't know. They are air lifting him into Cincinnati, Ohio Critical Care Hospital."

Then fear gripped me, I went into hyperventilation, and fainted. My father-in-law caught me and I could hear him scream, "Someone help her." I don't know how long they worked with me.

This was time for Tom to take over and he did. He got the phone and got all the information, and called my other children. They put me in the car, and we headed out for Indiana. Then he began to speak unto them in parables, a certain man planted a vineyard and set an hedge about it, and dug a place for the wine vat and built a tower and let it out to husbandmen and went into a far country." Mark 12:1 KJV.

Garfield and his family had planned a hunting trip with my brother, Merle, through the Thanksgiving Holidays. As they were coming back from hunting, my brother, Merle, who at the time was thirty-six years old, was driving and had a stroke. They proceeded and hit a brick culvert, and his truck flipped six times.

Garfield, who had unfastened his seat belt to secure his 13 year old son that was lying asleep in the back seat, was ejected from the truck. He flew through the air 155 feet, hitting a tree, breaking multiple bones, and injuring his brain. His son Merle (my brother's name sake) only sustained one scratch on his nose.

They had to call the jaws-of-life to my brother to cut him out. This accident left him with injuries that would leave him to never be able to work at his job again.

Garfield needed much more medical attention, surgeries and rehabilitation. And with prayer, he has somewhat fully recovered. He still has a limp in his right hip, leg and foot.

Garfield and his wife Rebecca and children, are now traveling in the ministry, telling how good God is. This is a story to be told, by Garfield, himself.

Top Row: Garfield Chambers, Merle Seeley,
James Seeley, Jimmy Dalton

Bottom: Garfield Seeley, Garfield Chambers IV,
Merle Chambers

For more information about Edith's story,
the Pye family, or the latest news and events;
please contact them at

edithpye@gmail.com

This is a book based upon encouragement and illustrates that God still works miracles and can change situations through the power of prayer.

About the Author

I was born in London Kentucky to a wonderful couple named Clarence and Jeanette Seeley. When I was three weeks old we moved to Indiana where I shared my home and childhood with twelve other siblings.

Our dad was a Pentecostal preacher who traveled from state to state. We were at home alone with our mother a lot, who did the best she could to raise us from the bible. She was a strong willed woman of faith. Dad died at the age of 76 but thank God we still have our mom.

When I turned 22, I married a preacher of the same faith. We repeated the same lifestyle as my parents. We lived in Ohio until our first son, Garfield Jr., was born. When he turned six weeks old we moved to Atlanta Georgia to start a ministry, (Faith Church of God).

God added three more precious children to our family with Gary Wayne, Tamatha Violet and Gregory Paul. All four children were born with many serious illnesses. They were all born with asthma and severe allergies. Our youngest son suffered the most. We spent many a night at the hospital with our children, praying and asking God to keep them and heal them. There was much heartache and tears, but more than that we had much joy.

As Gregory, our youngest son, turned nineteen months old we stopped pastoring the church and started traveling in the ministry. We traveled for many years with our children by our side. We lost their father when he turned 67.

Today, our four children are grown and now have families of their own. God has blessed us with four children and fourteen grandchildren.